THIS BOOK IS ABOUT

PREPARED WITH LOVE,
BY

Other Exley giftbooks:
In Praise & Celebration of Daughters
To a very special Son
Welcome to the New Baby
Our Family Record Book
A Grandmother's Record Book

Published simultaneously in 1997 by Exley Publications in Great Britain, and Exley Publications LLC in the USA.

12 11 10 9 8 7 6 5

ILLUSTRATIONS BY ANGELA KERR

Copyright © Helen Exley 1997.

ISBN 1-85015-947-5

Edited and written by Helen Exley.
Typeset by Delta, Watford.
Printed in China.

**Exley Publications Ltd,
16 Chalk Hill, Watford,
Herts WD19 4BG,
United Kingdom.**

**Exley Publications LLC,
185 Main Street, Spencer,
MA 01562, USA.**

www.helenexleygiftbooks.com

INTRODUCTION

Here is a journal that enables you to keep a record of some of the most amazing and joyful experiences in life – the first weeks and years of a child's existence!

Write down the events as they occur – all those happy, chaotic and hilarious moments. Then, later on, you will be able to focus on this time in your life and relive it all with a smile. Babies are babies for such a short time. Enjoy it and remember to record everything. Glue in lots of photographs and your child's first drawings, and rewrite headings so that they're relevant to you.

This book will make a precious memento for both you and your child – and perhaps, one day, even for your grandchildren.

Helen Exley

Baby Record Book

ILLUSTRATED BY
ANGELA KERR

EXLEY

Contents

The birth	7
First visitors	7
What your arrival meant to us	8
Family tree	9
Your mother	10
Your father	11
A message to you	11
Messages from your grandparents	12
The world when you were born	13
Our home	14
Your room	15
Firsts in the early months	16
Funny moments	16
Mementos	17
Things to remember	17
Outings	18
Your best-loved things	18
Growth chart	19
Tooth chart	19
Medical records	20
Immunizations	20
One very special day	21
Your first longer journeys	21
Celebrations! festivals! parties! fun!	22
Our family	24
More milestones	25
First sounds and words	25
One year old	26
After one year – the things you most loved	28
A typical day	30
Milestones as you grew	32
The worst times	33
Talents and interests as you grew	34
Early writing	36
Early drawings	38
First school-days	40
Your early hopes and ambitions	41
Important events of your childhood	42
The things you said!	43
Things we'll always remember	44

The Birth

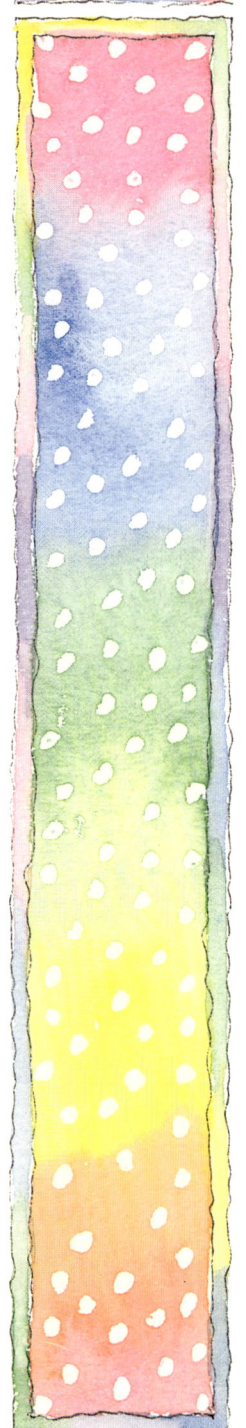

PLACE

DATE   TIME

WEIGHT   LENGTH

WHAT YOU LOOKED LIKE

THINGS WE WILL NEVER FORGET

First Visitors

WHAT THEY SAID

MESSAGES, GIFTS AND FLOWERS

What Your Arrival Meant To Us

FOR A PHOTO

Family Tree

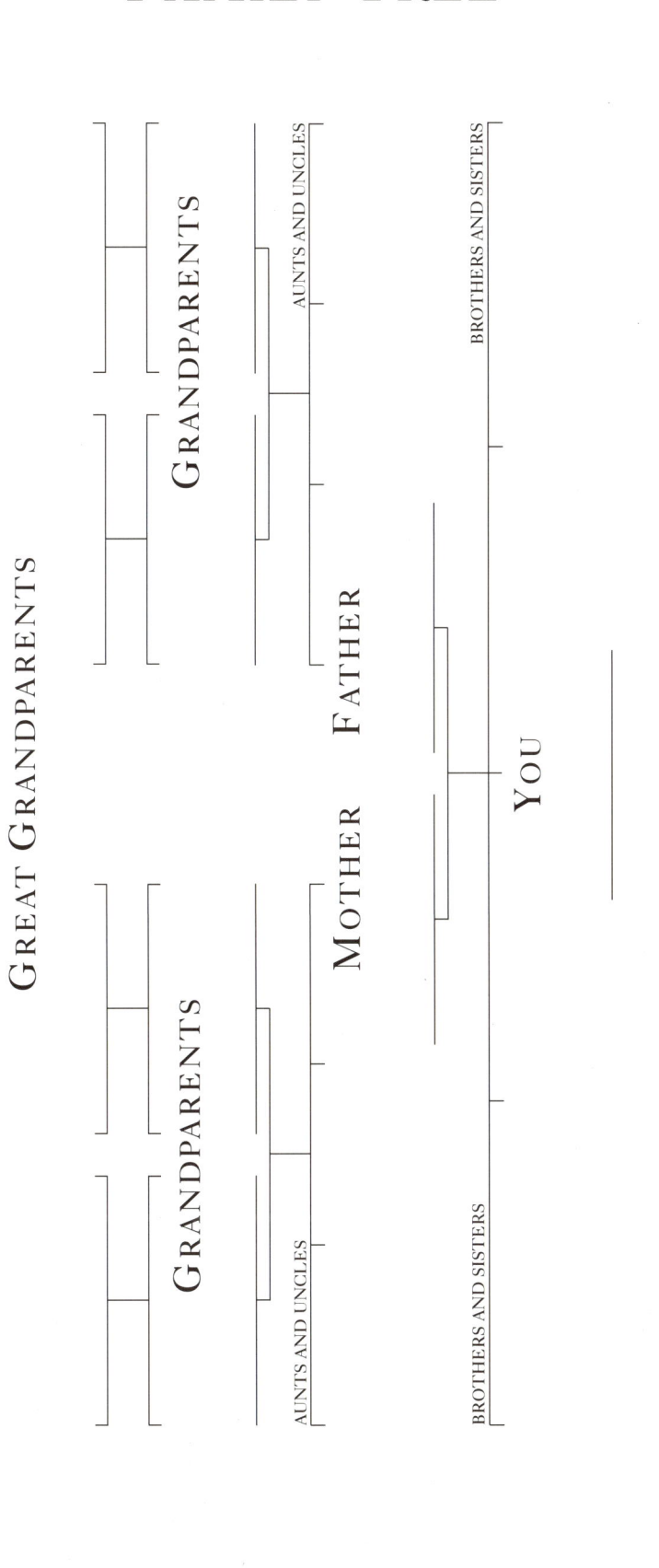

Great Grandparents

Grandparents

Grandparents

Aunts and Uncles

Aunts and Uncles

Mother   Father

Brothers and Sisters

Brothers and Sisters

You

Your Mother

HER EARLY LIFE, HOW YOUR COMING CHANGED HER LIFE

HER DREAMS AND HOPES FOR YOU

FOR A PHOTO OF MOTHER AND FATHER

Your Father

SOMETHING ABOUT HIS LIFE BEFORE YOU CAME, WHAT YOUR COMING MEANT TO HIM

WHAT HE HOPES FOR YOU

A Message To You

Messages From Your Grandparents

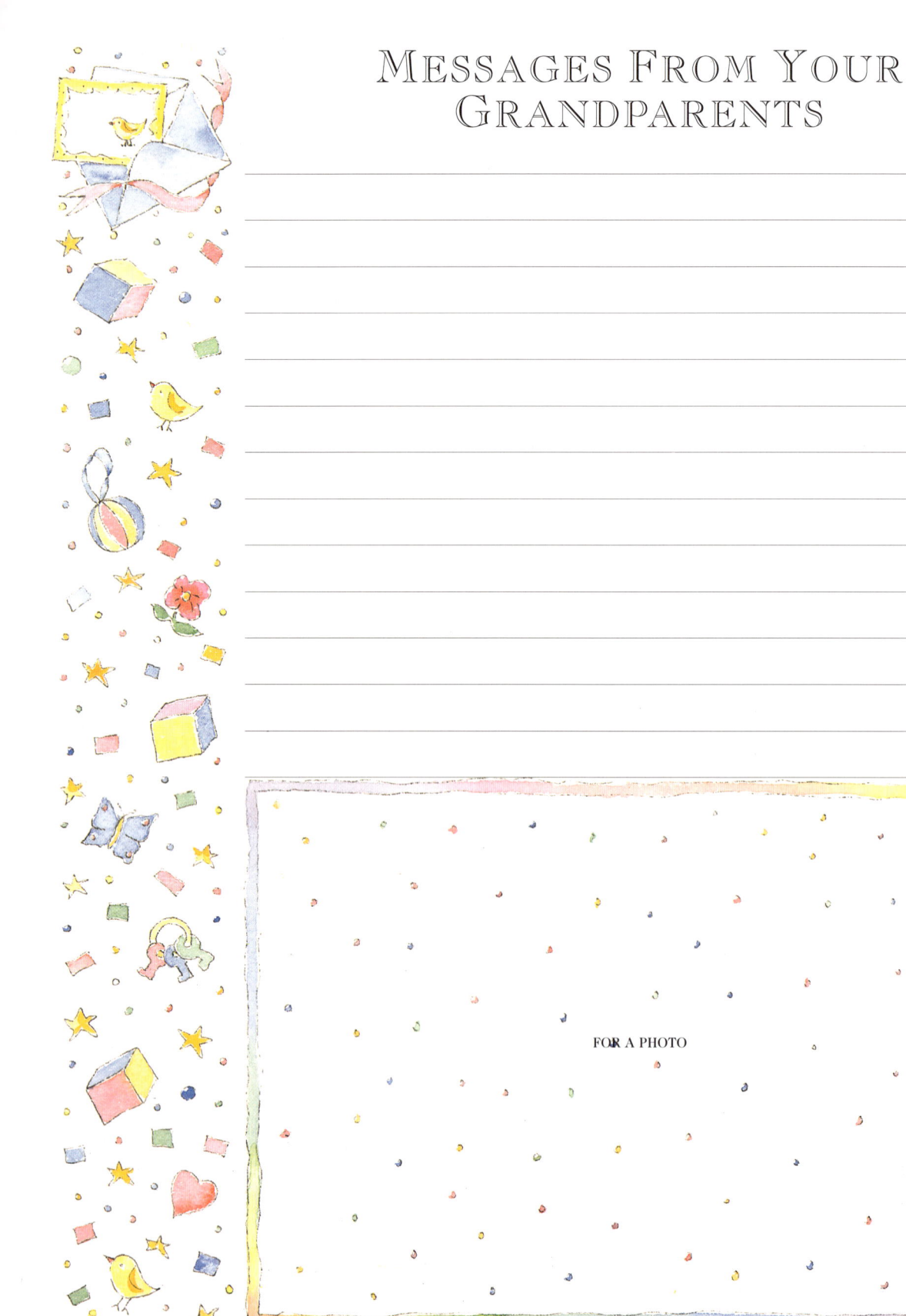

FOR A PHOTO

The World When You Were Born

PRESS CLIPPINGS, INSTEAD OF PHOTOGRAPHS, COULD BE ADDED HERE

Our Home

Your Room

Firsts In The Early Months

GRASPED A FINGER

HELD HEAD UP

RECOGNIZED A PARENT'S VOICE

RECOGNIZED YOUR OWN NAME

SMILED

DISCOVERED YOUR OWN HANDS

SUCKED YOUR THUMB

ATE SOLID FOODS

OTHERS

Funny Moments

Mementos

| A LOCK OF HAIR | YOUR FOOTPRINT | YOUR HANDPRINT |

don't forget the dates!

Things To Remember

OUTINGS

PLACES YOU REMEMBER

FIRST VISITS TO RELATIVES, THE SEA, THE FOREST, A FAIRGROUND...

PLACES AND THINGS THAT DELIGHTED YOU

TIMES WHEN IT ALL WENT WRONG!

YOUR BEST-LOVED THINGS

PEOPLE, TOYS, SONGS, RHYMES, MUSIC – ANYTHING AND EVERYTHING

Growth Chart

AGE	HEIGHT	WEIGHT
ONE WEEK		
ONE MONTH		
TWO MONTHS		
THREE MONTHS		
SIX MONTHS		
ONE YEAR		
EIGHTEEN MONTHS		
TWO YEARS		
THREE YEARS		
FOUR YEARS		
FIVE YEARS		

Tooth Chart

1ST TOOTH	UPPER	11TH
2ND		12TH
3RD		13TH
4TH		14TH
5TH		15TH
6TH	LEFT / RIGHT	16TH
7TH		17TH
8TH		18TH
9TH		19TH
10TH	LOWER	20TH

A CHILD WILL HAVE 20 TEETH – YOU CAN RECORD AND LABEL WHEN EACH OF THESE TEETH APPEARS.

Medical Records

DOCTOR'S VISITS　　　　　　　　　　　　　　　　　　　　　　　DATE

ILLNESSES

ALLERGIES

BLOOD GROUP

OTHER IMPORTANT INFORMATION

Immunizations

VERY IMPORTANT! KEEP ACCURATE DETAILS FOR FUTURE REFERENCE

IMMUNIZATION

MEASLES

POLIO

TETANUS

WHOOPING COUGH

OTHERS

One Very Special Day

FOR A CHRISTENING OR NAMING DAY, OR AN IMPORTANT HAPPY DAY FOR THE FAMILY

Your First Longer Journeys

VISITS TO GRANDPARENTS, WEEKEND TRIPS, OVERSEAS TRAVEL...

Celebrations! Festivals! Parties! Fun!

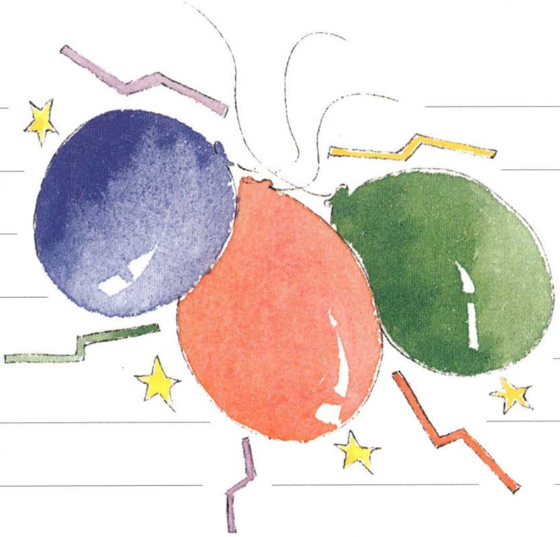

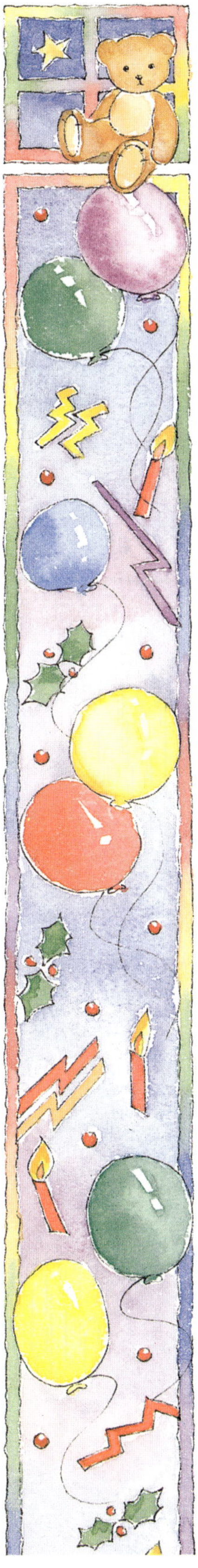

Our Family

TRADITIONS, WHAT WE ARE LIKE, WHAT WE DO, WHAT WE ENJOY...

More Milestones

FIRST LAUGHED OUT LOUD

FIRST WAVED BYE-BYE

FIRST RECOGNIZED YOURSELF IN THE MIRROR

FIRST ROLLED OVER

FIRST CRAWLED

FIRST SAT UP UNSUPPORTED

OTHER IMPORTANT FIRSTS

First Sounds And Words

RECORDING THE DATES COULD BE IMPORTANT, TOO

One Year Old

FOR A PHOTO

After One Year - The Things You Most Loved

STORIES, SONGS, GAMES, FRIENDS...

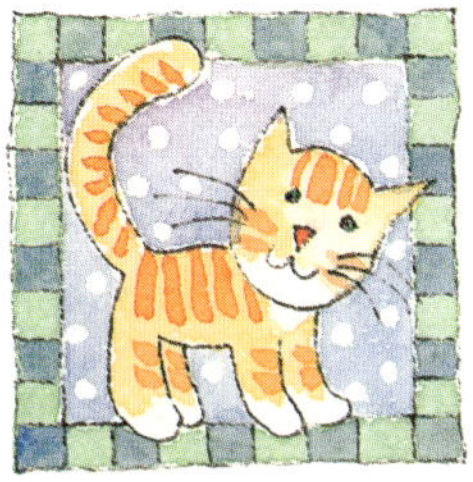
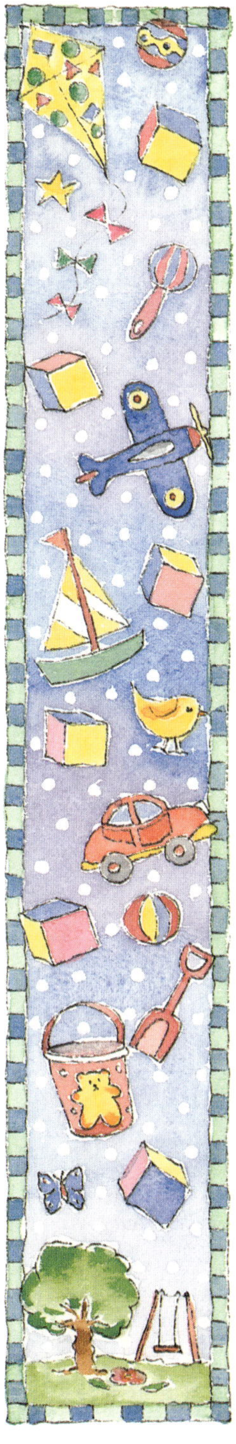
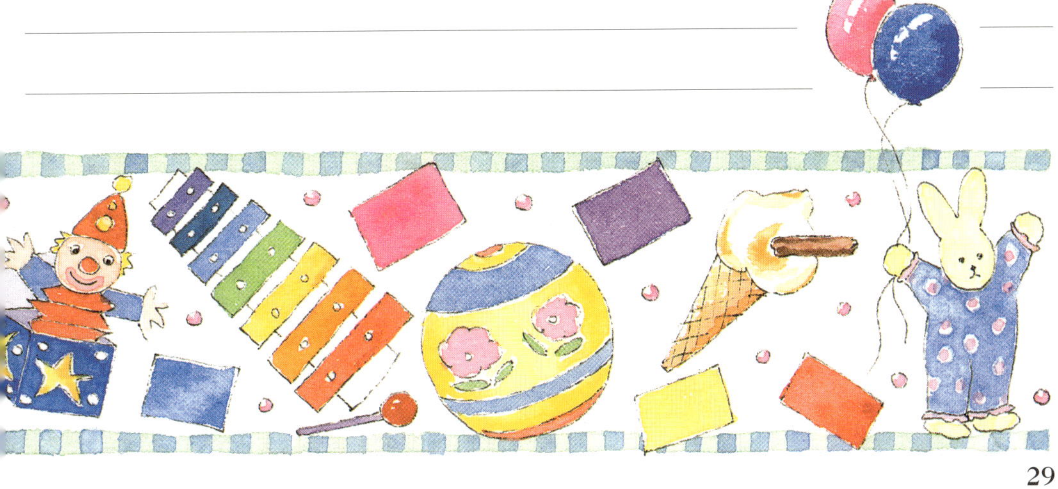

A Typical Day

AND LITTLE THINGS WE LOVED DOING TOGETHER

FOR A PHOTO

MILESTONES AS YOU GREW

The Worst Times

THINGS THAT FRIGHTENED YOU

THINGS YOU HATED

ACCIDENTS AND DISASTERS

SAD EVENTS

YOUR FIRST MISCHIEF – AND PUNISHMENT

Talents And Interests As You Grew

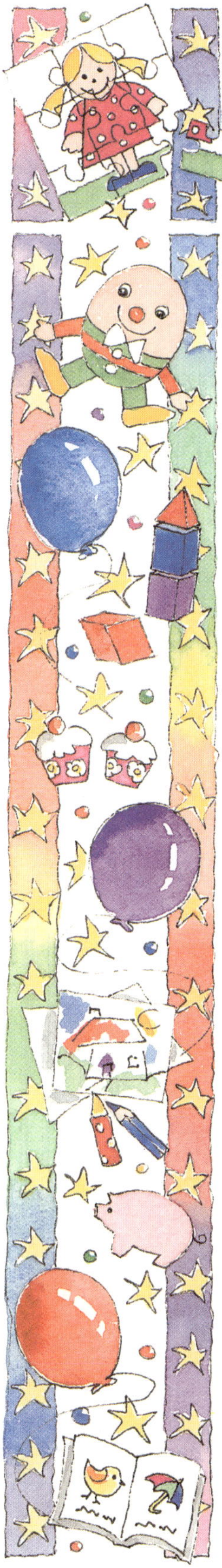

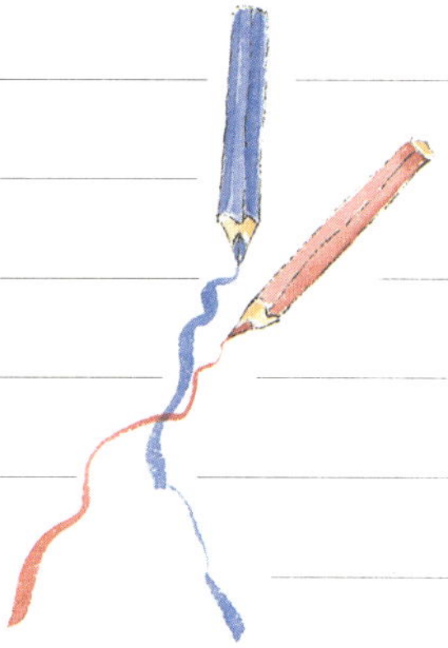

Early Writing

GLUE THE BEST EXAMPLES HERE

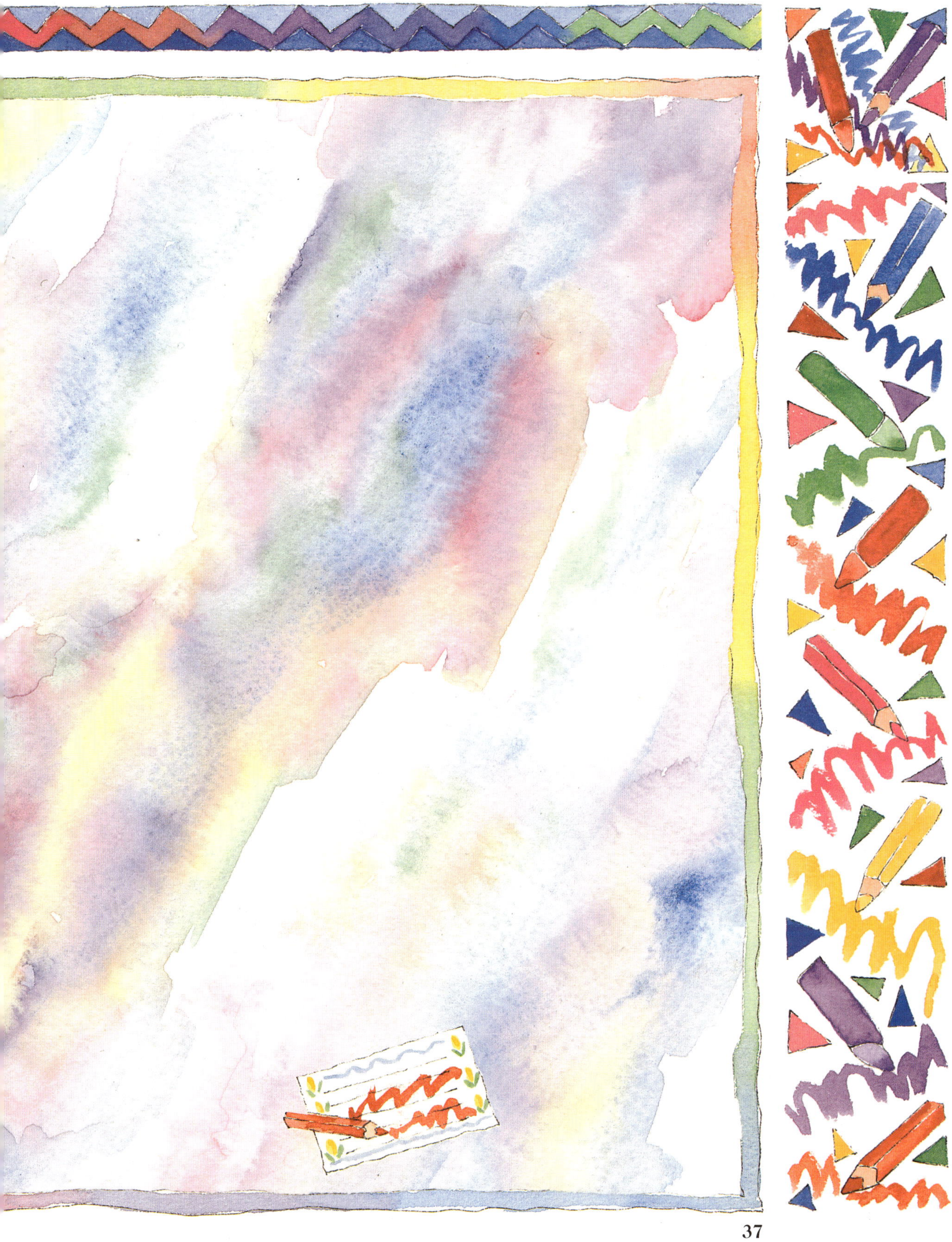

Early Drawings

39

First School-Days

YOUR FIRST DAY

YOUR TEACHERS

SUBJECTS YOU LOVED

SUBJECTS YOU HATED

OTHER IMPORTANT THINGS IN SCHOOL

Your Early Hopes and Ambitions

EARLY GOALS AND DREAMS

ACHIEVEMENTS

DIFFICULTIES YOU OVERCAME

Important Events Of Your Childhood

THE THINGS YOU SAID!

ALL SMALL CHILDREN COME OUT WITH DELIGHTFUL OR OUTRAGEOUS THINGS – HERE ARE SOME OF YOURS

Things We'll Always Remember

PARENTS, GRANDPARENTS AND PEOPLE WHO LOVE YOU COULD WRITE MEMORIES AND MESSAGES HERE

Notes, Photographs, Mementos...